The Museum of Missing Things

by

Ellen Estilai

The Museum of Missing Things

To the memory of my parents

Kenneth and Gloria Andrus Price

In *The Museum of Missing Things,* Ellen Estilai brings her painter's eye to the page, rendering a memoir-in-moments at various turns poignant, witty, and harrowing. Readers will find miniatures magnified, illuminated by Estilai's interior awareness and connected by her attention to overlapping palimpsests of language, relationships, geography, and cultural history. Such a beautiful, moving book.

--Jo Scott-Coe,
author of *Unheard Witness:*
The Life and Death of Kathy Leissner Whitman

Table of Contents

On Indefinite Loan to the Universe: Empty Spaces from the Permanent Collection, Museum of Missing Things

Curator's statement:

All empty spaces in this exhibition have been set aside for the juvenilia, artwork, unpublished manuscripts, and ephemera reported missing by Ellen Estilai, artist/author (American, b. 1947). While we are at the mercy of Estilai's incomplete recollections, enough memory fragments exist to give us a picture of her early creative evolution and some insight into the causes of the relatively fallow period of her middle years.

The Museum of Missing Things wishes to acknowledge the Islamic Republic of Iran, without whose zeal Estilai's graduate school paper on *To the Lighthouse* would not remain unavailable to us.

Catalogue No.   18302.10
Paper Doll Geishas, crayon on paper, c. 1953.

Artist's statement:

I made the paper doll geishas when I was staying home from second grade in Seattle. I had bronchitis or tonsillitis almost every Monday, so I missed more days of school than I attended, but that just gave me more time to make art. I took these dolls with me to my doctor's office and proudly showed them off to her, chattering on about their life stories, their elaborate hairdos, and my design choices—pastel chrysanthemums on vibrant blue, red and violet kimonos. The doctor smiled and nodded politely at first, but soon her eyes began to go somewhere else inside her head and her smile got panicky around the corners of her mouth. My embarrassed mother told me we were not there to talk about paper dolls. "This is not the right time," she said.

When would have been the right time—before or after I threw up on the doctor's shoes?

That day in the doctor's office, I realized that art, specifically my art, could be embarrassing, like throwing up. I learned to be careful.

Catalogue No. 19568.12
Pretty Lady, watercolor on paper, c. 1960.

Artist's statement:

I made Pretty Lady when I was in 7th grade in Pomona, California. It's one of a series of pretty ladies I painted between 1951 and 1965, before my neo-Dada, Bay Area Funk professors at UC Davis taught me to "paint ugly." However, this pretty lady was different from the others in the series. She was so pretty she was grotesque—or so I thought. Of course, while I was painting her, I loved her. She was Snow White, Maid Marion, Princess Soraya, Vivian Leigh, and my mother. I could be this lady someday! I gave her dark, wavy hair, pink cheeks, red lips, and a tiny waist, accentuated by an enormous embroidered skirt that took up half the page. I filled the brilliant green lawn under her skirt with flowers, delineating with fearless strokes every blade of grass, every flower petal, reveling in the frenzy of lines and textures—not delicate transparent layers, but thick, brash slashes.

When I was finished, Pretty Lady's eyes stared at me from a frenetic, cacophonous composition that I didn't recognize as mine. This wasn't what I had planned. Somehow, I had wandered out of the Backyard of the Subtle and Decorous and into the Garden of the Unseemly and Inappropriate. *I'm in an unfamiliar neighborhood, and I'd better get home before dark.*

I brought Pretty Lady to school the next day, but I couldn't bring myself to show it to my art teacher. She tried to persuade me, but she was too polite to insist. I wanted her to insist. I wanted her to tell me my painting was not outrageous—or that it was okay to be outrageous. I kept the painting in my book bag, too embarrassed to take a chance, too cowardly to honor the work.

Sylvia Plath said, "The worst enemy to creativity is self-doubt," and who would know better than Sylvia Plath? She wrote this in a letter to herself in 1953, when she was just twenty-one, nine years before that self-doubt filled up her lungs and seeped into her brain, putting an end to her creativity.

I would like to have Pretty Lady back, to see what it was that my thirteen-year-old self found so humiliating. But more than anything, I would like to see if I could paint that way again.

Catalogue No. 19736.05

Untitled (Character Study of Terri B., Friend of the Author), ballpoint pen on three-hole punch, lined paper, c. 1963.

Artist's statement:

"Write a character study of someone," said Mr. Richards, "without using any physical description of your subject." That assignment was a challenge for high school juniors, for whom physical appearance was everything. Appearance provided the context and structure of our days, fodder for our gossip, and fuel for our angst. Physiognomy was destiny, and so was the length of our skirts.

However, as obsessed as I was with physical appearance, mine and everyone else's, I had no trouble choosing a subject for this exercise. My friend Terri's bedroom abounded with clues to her character. The rumpled clothes, bubble gum wrappers, and matted hairbrushes provided a roadmap to her soul. The essay practically wrote itself.

Well, almost. I labored over it obsessively, taking words out, putting them back in, moving phrases around until they had the right rhythm, until the surface chaos of Terri's room had a deeper sense of order and purpose.

I can remember only two phrases from that page-and-a-half of tightly written description: "a clandestine copy of Mad Magazine" and "dusty pork rinds under the bed." I'm sure I got extra points for "clandestine," an SAT-worthy word that hadn't yet appeared on our vocabulary lists.

When I read my essay in class, one of the students asked me how long it took me to write it. "Several days," I said.

"Well, it seemed like it just flowed out of you all at once," she replied.

Rats! I had just revealed my sweaty little secret. I should have said I had written it in one sitting. Then I would have seemed like a natural writer, a real writer. I'd blown my chance at coolness yet again.

When I write now, I know the best I can do is make it seem easy. Appearance is everything.

Catalogue No. 19822.16

Conversation: Portrait of the Artist with Mother and Father, acrylic on canvas, 1964

Artist's statement:

Just before I started my senior year of high school, just when I was beginning to think that maybe I could be one of the cool girls, my family moved from Pomona to Sacramento. My parents rented a house with a guest cottage/studio where I spent all my time when I wasn't in school. The studio was filled with light, thanks to the floor-to-ceiling windows on the north and south sides. Occasionally, an over-confident quail would fly in through an open window and thump into the opposite wall of glass, falling into a soft heap in the middle of the floor. I would have to stop painting and get a shovel to remove it. But most of the time, I worked uninterrupted, late into the night.

That was the loneliest year of my life and one of the most creative. At my new high school, three outsider bo-hemians befriended me, but I missed my network of Pomona friends. I found solace in a clean, well-lighted place where I could make art—a room of one's own. I produced so much work that my art teacher, Mr. Coates, told me that I was more professional than he was. He wasn't talking about the quality so much as the sheer volume.

I made *Conversation* late in my senior year. In this painting, my mother, my father and I are sitting around a table, talking intently—something we rarely did without incident. As usual, I am focused on my mother, and my father is looking on. The relationship of the figures to one another is ambiguous, but I think I may have been trying to capture that moment just before I got too comfortable and said the thing that would make my mother leave the room. The figures are large and ungainly, reminiscent of that mid-western neo-mannerist, Thomas Hart Benton. I didn't particularly like Benton. It was just that I wasn't much of a draftsman. That didn't bother Mr. Coates, who liked the painting well enough to haul it 35 miles or so to Lodi and enter it in the annual Art and Wine Festival exhibition. The reporter from the local TV station must have liked it too, because a few days later, we saw it on the evening newscast.

My parents kept the painting for me when I went away to college, taking it with them when they moved back to Southern California. I know it was hanging in the living room when I came home for school holidays, and it was still there while I was living in Iran, but after the Iranian Revolution, when my family and I sought temporary shelter at my parents' house, it was gone.

"What happened to that painting of the three of us," I asked my father, dreading the answer.

"Your mother got rid of it."

"How? Did she take a knife to it?"

He smiled and nodded.

One of my subjects had sashayed out of the canvas and ripped it to shreds. Everybody's a critic.

I was not surprised. I'm not sure what set her off that time. Maybe she didn't like the draftsmanship or the ambiguity or the invasion of her privacy. Perhaps she had invented a dialogue for the conversation and didn't like what she heard. Maybe she regretted not having that clean, well-lighted place, that room of her own—or a college degree.

It's not just the painting I miss; it's the opportunity. I could have asked my father why he hadn't tried to stop her. I could have asked my mother why she did it. I could have reminded her that it wasn't hers to destroy.

Now that would have been a conversation.

Catalogue No. 25336.64
Untitled (House Covered with Flowers), ceramic, 1969

12

Artist's Statement:

All those flowers that embarrassed me so much in 7th grade found their way into this ceramic sculpture, made in Robert Arneson's class at UC Davis. I make no apologies for them. They were over the top, and that's just where they belonged. Sure, the flowers were creamy pastels, but they swallowed up the little cottage in a fierce tangle of stamens, pistils, and tendrils—straight from the Garden of the Unseemly and Inappropriate.

This piece was selected for a student show at the Memorial Union on campus. The Iranian graduate student with molten brown eyes who would later become my husband knew only my first name, but he knew I had a piece in the show. When he went to the gallery to find out my last name, he saw there were two Ellens. Fortunately, he looked up the right one in the phone book.

Catalogue No. 37916.18
Graduate School paper on *To The Lighthouse*, c. 1977.

Artist's Statement:

I wrote this paper for Nahid Sarmad's 20th Century American Novel class at the University of Tehran. Somehow, it wasn't among the cache of my graduate school essays that I found in my brother-in-law's basement when I went back to Iran in 2008. I wish I still had this essay because, when Nahid handed it back to me, she said, "You know, I was up all night grading these papers, and it was 2:30 in the morning when I came to yours. You wrote, 'So much depends on distance.'"

And here, I wish I could remember exactly what I had written. I know I was repeating the narrator's phrase to make some point about the distance between the letters "A" and "R," the distance to the lighthouse, the distance between the characters.... Whatever I wrote, it kept Nahid from nodding off on her pile of essays. "It cheered me so much," she said. "You're a writer, and it's undeveloped."

At least, that's how I think she put it. Never mind that the pronoun "it" had no referent. That's how I've told this story to myself at odd moments when Nahid pops into my head, when I'm organizing the sock drawer or alphabetizing the spices, or mopping cilantro slime from the bottom of the crisper—anything to avoid writing. That missing referent probably had more to do with Nahid's lack of sleep than any unfamiliarity with the language. She spoke impeccable, elegant English, perfected while doing her doctoral research at NYU.

You're a writer, and it's undeveloped. She looked straight at me, challenging me when she said it, as if she knew I had been avoiding it. It.

I had always hoped I would see Nahid again and thank her for those words, but that's impossible now. I suspected her death a few years ago while reading a former colleague's memoir. The author wrote about their friendship with a sad finality. She had given Nahid a pseudonym, but I immediately recognized her passionate morality, her earnest loyalty. It took me longer to actually absorb the bad news. A year later, I asked another mutual friend if he had heard from Nahid. He said, "I think she's…dead." He looked at me strangely as if to say, how could you have read that memoir and not known that?

The only way I can reach Nahid now is via Google, that medium I call upon late at night to conjure up the missing, neglected, and departed. When I Googled her, I learned that the American poet Karen Swenson had dedicated a poem to her. It begins,

"I have lost the address of my country," my friend says, her voice soft in her mouth as barefoot dust on the streets of Persepolis and Bam—dust baked to the hard bricks of old mosques.

"I have lost the address of my country." That sounds like something Nahid would have said. In fact, I may even have heard her say it the last time we saw each other, over thirty years ago in Berkeley, after the Iranian revolution, when she was debating whether or not to return home.

I have lost the address of my friend. But if I could find her, I would tell her that I am a writer, and it's developing.

Persian Lessons

Lesson I: The Indefinite –i (Persian Grammar, A.K.S. Lambton, p. 3)

It was my need to belong that drove me to learn Persian. I prided myself on my command of the idiom. The secret to my steep learning curve was pretending. Make-believe was my major strategy. I was not content to merely memorize verb conjugations and the uses of the subjunctive. My tactic early on was to convince myself that I was Iranian. Even before I had the vocabulary, I had mastered the cadence of a Persian sentence. I watched other women carefully and adopted their subtle body language. That first month in Te hran, I willed myself to dream in Persian. Leaving Iran nine ye ars later, after the revolution, I felt like a foreigner, but I also felt like a displaced Iranian.

Lesson VI: The Passive Voice (p. 53)
Formation of the negative:

Koshte nashodam
I was not killed

17

Koshte nashode am
I have not been killed

Koshte nakhaham shod
I shall not be killed

I had formed a special bond with Salman, the neighborhood grocer.
I was his only foreign customer. I think he liked me because I had
bothered to learn Persian. He also seemed to appreciate my
childishly scrawled Persian shopping lists. So even when there
were shortages—and there were many—he managed to set
something aside for me—a few eggs or a small box of laundry
detergent. If other people were in the store, he would scratch his
stubbly beard and say, "*Nah, Khanum* (madam). We're out of
detergent today." But he would fix his gaze at me just a second
longer than necessary and raise one eyebrow almost imperceptibly.
I would know then that I should come back when the other
customers had gone, and he would have ready a small box of Tide
neatly wrapped in brown paper.

As anti-American sentiment increased, others had become less
accepting. The usually friendly woman across the street suddenly
stopped returning my salaam. And one day, when I called the

Butane Gas Company to order another canister for the stove, the agent taking my order interrupted me to ask, "*Khanum*, are you a foreigner?"

At the Tehran Museum of Contemporary Art, where I worked, I answered a phone call one day from an Iranian woman who wanted some information about current exhibitions. Before hanging up, she asked, "Is this a museum for foreigners?" "Not at all," I assured her. "It's Iranian. "*Manzel e khodetoon e.*" This is your home.

The museum did belong to the people, but in reality it housed two cultures existing side by side. It was not just a matter of Iranian artists sharing space on the walls with their European and American counterparts; it was also the museum's western-educated administrative and curatorial staff working among the more traditional and religious support staff. Soon I would see that, for those in the latter group, the museum, in its current form, would never be their home.

One afternoon, a museum guard found a note stuck in the frame of Tom Wesselmann's *Great American Nude,* a stylized painting of a big, blowsy blonde whose most predominate feature was bright pink nipples. The note said, "Next time, this will be a bomb."

Lesson VI: The Subjunctive Present after certain conjunctions (p.60)

Translation exercise
1. As long as the children are here, you must stay.   2. In spite of the fact that he wanted to go, he was unable to do so.   3. It is impossible to go.   4. He ought to have gone yesterday.   6. We ought to have gone the day before yesterday.

One night I dreamed that Ali and I were sitting in a quintessential New Yorker cartoon living room: matching stodgy armchairs, a floor lamp casting a pale golden light, French doors leading to a terrace—a comfy, middle-class tableau. We sat facing each other, engrossed in our newspapers. Just outside the French doors, I could hear our daughters screaming. People were beating them, but Ali and I paid no attention. We continued to read as their screams grew louder.

"Should we do something?" I asked.

"There is nothing we can do," he said.

Lesson XIII: Uses of the Subjunctive

in kar ra hala bekonid ta zudtar tamam shavad (p. 151)
Do this now so that it will be finished sooner
ta doulat ha in tour bashand ouza khub namishavad
As long as the governments are like this conditions will not improve. (p. 159)

After dessert, while the children played indoors, we sat outside on the terrace of our friends' house drinking tea and enjoying the soft, balmy night, bright with shooting stars. The shortwave radio was playing in the background, tuned to the BBC World Service—its tinny, bottom-of-the-well sound offering a familiar counterpoint to our conversation. As we   frequently did that summer, we talked about leaving: *Do we really have to leave? For how long? What will happen to our lives here? What if we were to stay?*

We were only half-listening to the radio when we heard,

"Today in Kerman…." We all leaned closer. "…four people were stoned to death." We stared at the radio in disbelief. Hangings and firing squads were becoming everyday occurrences, but stoning?

"Sexual offences…prostitution… two men and two women."

After a summary trial, the prisoners were placed in holes dug expressly for their execution and buried up to their chests. Sacks were placed over their heads, and five especially chosen people— one of them the presiding judge of a revolutionary court—began throwing stones. We heard later from a nephew in Kerman that one of these five executioners was the son of one of the women.

In my dream, Ali had said there was nothing we could do. But Iranians say that women dream the opposite of reality. If we were not convinced before that we needed to leave Iran, we were certain now.

Lesson XIV: Polite Conversation

(p. 169) A variety of expressions are used upon taking leave. On wishing to terminate a meeting or visit it is customary to ask one's host's permission to leave by some such phrase as morrakhas mifarmaid *or* ejaze mifarmaid, *"do you give me permission to depart" or by indicating that one has troubled one's host long enough by a phrase such as* zahmat kam konam, *"let me make the trouble (given by me) less."*

At Mehrabad Airport, the officer behind the counter hands Ali my and our children's passport. Then he disappears into an adjoining room to look for Ali's. He comes back empty-handed, except for an official-looking envelope that he gives to Ali. Ali is very quiet. I move over to the counter and stand next to him as the officer leafs through a huge ledger with neatly handwritten entries.

"You're on the list, sir," he says to Ali.

"OK, that's great," I say.

Ali is very pale. He doesn't look at me as he says, "That's the *mamnou'ol khorouj* list."

Mamnou'ol khorouj. Exit prohibited.

Album of Photos Taken and Never Taken

26

<u>Claremont, California, circa 2005 (or anytime between 1955 and 2008):</u>
My father tells me my mother smiled at something he said today. To mark the occasion, I take this mental snapshot, underexposed, milky black and white. She is silhouetted against the window in front of the herb garden she has let die. Her eyes are fixed on the columns of solitaire cards fanned out on the Formica dining table, a corner of her mouth turned up in a barely perceptible smile. He is walking out of the frame, beaming, pleased with himself.

Ellwood City, Pennsylvania, circa 1952:

In a memory borrowed from my mother, I stand in the doorway of the Yahn-Jones Hardware Store, the afternoon light at my back, and look deep into the cool darkness, down the long aisle flanked by wooden display cases where my mother is standing behind the counter, making the black and gold cash register jingle. I have never seen her without me before. When I cry out, "Mommy, you are so beautiful!" she turns to look at me. Her smile, like the Cheshire Cat's, is suspended in the dark air above the marble countertop. I love when she reads me the Cheshire Cat story. It's not the grin that tugs at me; it's the fading away.

<u>Wiley Hill, Ellwood City, Pennsylvania, circa 1948</u>:

My parents stand in front of the GI Bill house, a log cabin covered with tarpaper shingles. I'm in my stroller, the replacement baby. It's a tiny snapshot, but I can tell that only my father is smiling. Not bothering to pose, my mother wears her housewife frock with resolute indifference. Her hair is tied back carelessly, wisps escaping in what I will come to recognize as the beginning of resignation and martyrdom.

32

<u>Washington, DC, April 1947:</u>

My mother took this picture of my father holding a newly arrived me, his firstborn, swaddled in a receiving blanket on the front steps of their apartment building. She didn't need to tell him to smile. Somewhere, outside the frame, in this same city, maybe only a few blocks away, there is another first-born, another man's little girl my father doesn't know about, sixteen months and twenty-seven days older than me and given up for adoption.

<u>Ellwood City, Pennsylvania, December 1945:</u>

I almost don't recognize them--The Best Boy Dancer, Class of 1937, and the Prettiest Girl, Class of 1938, side by side in front of a clumsy but earnest, almost vaudevillian backdrop--a mottled tree trunk and hillside *sfumatto*. The photographer's lamp casts a warm glow from down low, like footlights, but Best and Prettiest are glowing from inside. He has just returned from a four-year tour in the European Theater of Operations. She has just returned from her own tour of duty, the where and why of which she will keep to herself. I almost don't recognize them because she has her arm draped casually around his shoulder, red lacquered nails against his hound's-tooth jacket—a gesture missing from six decades of photos, taken and never taken. He is smiling—a toothy, besotted grin. He cannot believe his good fortune. After four years in the hedgerows and trenches, he finds her still here, still waiting for him, still the Prettiest Girl. She wears a smart twill jacket and matching sweater—her Brenda Starr, Girl Reporter clothes—and an engagement ring on her right hand. Her blue-black hair falls in soft, effortless waves. She is smiling—a corner of her mouth turned up in a half-smile, one confident and secure, perhaps relieved, a smile even she might not have recognized sixty years from this day.

Walk-Ons

38

Scene One, Ellwood City, PA, 1951:

The small girl with tangled curls, her mother, and her kitten watch the neighbor's grandson play with his dog in the yard across the wire fence. The kitten crawls through a hole in the fence and makes its way through the tall, sweet summer grass to the boy and his dog. The boy picks up the kitten. The dog advances, barking, jumping. The boy drops the kitten in front of the dog. The girl and her mother watch as the dog tears the kitten apart.

"Look at its eyes!" cries the girl's mother.

Later, the boy will deny dropping the kitten. Years later the small girl will remember the first time she saw someone lie and get away with it.

Scene Two, Seattle, 1953:

The hall monitor is doing her job. She stands at the top of the stairs during recess and says to any child at the bottom of the stairs, "Whatareyoucomingupfor." The young girl with brown braids and a crooked part waits, scuffed shoe poised on the first step, her skinned knee bleeding. "Whatareyoucomingupfor," says the hall monitor.

The young girl, blood collecting in her white sock, climbs the stairs and walks past the hall monitor without answering. Years later, the girl will remember the day she understood that bureaucracy is unimaginative, and she will know that this knowledge is what she was coming up for.

41

Scene Three, San Francisco, 1967:

The man in the Greyhound bus station cafeteria sidles up to the young woman with long brown hair sitting alone, careless of her powers, eating a slice of apple pie. His stringy hair is slicked back, and he has fresh scratches on his face.

"I would like some pie," he says.

"I would like to be alone," she says.

Years later, she will wonder if the person who scratched him was even more careless than she.

Scene Four, San Francisco, 1967, later that same day:

The young woman with long brown hair, still careless of her powers, glides past the window of Caffe Trieste in North Beach. A thin man with a silk paisley cravat and a large boil on his nose dashes out of the café and asks her if she would like to come in for a coffee. Years later, the girl, now a woman with shorter brown hair and diminished powers, still wonders how men who wear cravats and carry warning signs on their faces can be so optimistic.

Scene Five, Los Angeles, 1971:

The young wife and her husband sit in the crowded LAX departure lounge watching a middle-aged man and woman with New York accents wage a loud argument. They play to the crowd. With every barb, like bad vaudeville actors, they sneak a peek at their audience and smile. Years later, the young wife, now middle-aged with hair that is no longer worth mentioning, will find herself in another airport lounge with that same husband, unsmiling, engaged in an argument for which she is relieved there is not much of an audience.

Scene Six, Ontario, CA, 1974:

In a different airport lounge, a tall, elegant young woman with long blonde hair, crisp blue blazer with gold buttons, and immaculate white pants, looks up from her magazine and says to the stranger sitting next to her: "Please put out that cigarette." He wastes no time grinding out the stub in the nearest ashtray while she turns back to her magazine. The youngish woman watching this encounter, having bypassed power suits on her journey from bohemian to matronly, knows that she would sooner move to another seat than make such a request. Years later, she will find her version of the voice that makes people do what they would rather not do, but she will never master the power suit.

Scene Seven, Toronto, 1990:

The old woman in a gray coat wheels around a Toronto street corner so fast she nearly runs into the young American woman and her family looking in the shop windows. "Move!" she growls. From this one syllable, the American woman knows that the old woman is Italian, her kitchen smells of anise, sausage and fried peppers, and her family is afraid of her. Years later, the American woman's kitchen often smells of anise, sausage, and fried peppers, but her family is not afraid of her.

Scene Eight, Paris, 1997:

The handsome flight attendant praises the American woman for studying French on the flight from LAX to Paris. While she reviews the subjunctive mood, he makes sure her wine glass is filled, jokes with her husband, makes them feel special. They connect. As the American woman and her husband leave the airport, they see the flight attendant enter a glass elevator. They smile at him as he ascends. He sees them but looks away. His shift is over. *C'ést la vie.* Years later, the woman realizes that when you let a language slip away, the subjunctive is the first thing to go.

Lines Composed upon Remembering the Laundry Room, Lockhaven Apartments, Ballard, Seattle, Washington, circa 1953, after William Wordsworth

Six decades have passed, spinning, tumbling across two continents, mountainous topography of clothes folded in pristine laundry rooms—yet still ten washer/dryers later I conjure up that fuzzy smell of warm lint, slimy bleach, soap powder caked and crusty on the alien countertop.

At first, unnerving, like all new Seattle smells—sea air saltwater sandbox with cat feces red rubber rain boots lunchroom too close to the restroom—but this smell, with familiarity, slowly comforted, a welcome catch at the back of the throat, a chestfull of scent, private solace in a public place.

I had no business in that gray spare space, no duty except to my own imagination. Uninviting yet alluring, it offered a retreat from catcalls and parental strife, enveloping me in its warm yeasty fragrance, alone except for Little LuLu and the troll under the bridge.

My current laundry room is sterilely satisfactory, bleach-banished, pH balanced, lint gently trapped, ultra-concentrated for high efficiency. Free and clear. No animal testing. No fragrance. No imagination.

But often, in some hotel courtyard, the laundry room door ajar, linty, soapy, bleachy miasma escaping, I yearn to have business there. Lured back to a safer place by terrycloth and percale funk and yeasty fecundity, I ache to go inside and get to work, to sort, cleanse, bleach, dry to bone-dry, fold, and stack to the ceiling. To know when something is finished.

Elegy for Cosmo Cool Cat

You sauntered in sideways, your crooked tail an unheeded warning that our life would be askew, awry, a cosmic chaos of screen doors shredded and sofa arms rent relentlessly, an extended catastasis in search of a climax, a concatenation of catastrophes.

Tuxedo cat, more Frank Sinatra than Cary Grant, more insouciant than innocent, more boho than tuxedo, your reputation preceded you—the snatching of sandwiches from the hands that fed you, the baiting of thugs in the parking lots of LA (not for you a city of angels), the scars and oozing sores. Just temporary, we thought, this exile to the suburbs away from your nemeses. "Of course, we'll take him," we said. "We'll save him from himself."

Nothing could contain you. You were a black and white blur in every doorway.

Our vet, who came to know you well, would smile and murmur, "Oh Cosmo, Cosmo, Cosmo," and stitch you up again. He tagged your chart: "Difficult Cat." Nail trimming technicians encircled you—two, three at a time they came—but were vanquished. "We tried. We really tried."

Our Thanksgiving Day entertainment, you tripped out on tryptophan, catatonic. Not sure what to wish for, we held a mirror to your muzzle. "No, still alive," we said on many more than nine Thanksgivings, far more than we bargained for, far more than the odds.

Vaulting across our sternums at midnight, clawing our heads at 4 a.m., pacing behind our pillows, you would not be ignored, single-minded, restless, reckless, insatiable. Food when you wanted it, sliding door in and out and out and in and in and out when you wanted it. There was little to recommend you.

Little, except your heart, earnest and true, and that dog-like way you skipped along beside us, and the three or four hours after lights-out when you gave up your quest and nestled on top of us, or your last day, when you made your way to the cool shade of the mulberry tree. We still imagine you there, and in the doorways, a black and white blur, in and out and out and in and now out forever.

Saffron Prayers

My new favorite Persian word is *ghalambor*. It used to be *zaferaan*, or saffron, but after reading my friend Bahram's article on the *ney*, the reed plant, I am partial to *ghalambor*. It is a graft of two words, *ghalam*, a reed pen, and *bor*, from the verb *boridan*, to cut. A *ghalambor* is someone who, with a sharp knife and steady hand, fashions reeds into the pens used by a calligrapher.

I like the fluidity of *ghalambor*, the way it catches at the back of the soft palate in an uvular plosive—almost a gagging sound to the Western ear—then skims the alveolar ridge, and pauses between compressed lips before gliding out on that final, accented syllable—open, soft, unfettered by the final "r." *Ghalambor*.

It's my new favorite word as much for its sound as for the surprising obviousness of its meaning. The word is not even in my *Haïm's New Persian-English Dictionary*, but it should be. As much as I've admired the acrobatic, layered lines of Persian calligraphy, I never thought about the centuries of pen cutters who made them possible. Apparently, Mr. Haïm didn't either.

This oversight made me feel guilty and sad for the forgotten and marginalized *ghalambor*. It made me think of Rumi's poem about the Persian reed flute, cut from the same reed bed as the *ghalam*. Rumi says the flute's mournful sound is the cry of the reed longing to be reunited with its reed bed. Does the *ghalambor* long to be reunited with his pens? Does he long to write his own story?

This is the kind of melancholy that calls for saffron. *Zaferaan* and saffron, its softer English equivalent, are still favorite words—conjuring up languid Friday lunches with fragrant, steaming, saffron-laced rice. After years of cooking with saffron, I thought I knew all about it—how to grind it into a fine powder before dissolving it in hot water; how much to use before it becomes bitter and overwhelming; how, with the right person and the right paella, it's an aphrodisiac. I knew that the ancient Welsh used it to cure melancholy, and that Iranians believe too much of it could cause a person to die laughing. But from one of Bahram's books, I learned something else: to dispel unhappiness or grief, some devout Iranians write prayers in saffron ink, soak the prayer sheets in water, then drink the saffron-tinged liquid left behind.

The *ghalambor* should do this. The pen cutter should become the penman. He should grind the saffron the way a calligrapher would grind pigment for his ink. Inhaling the honey-sweet saltiness, he should steep the powder until the water turns sunset orange, then wet the sharpened reed he kept for himself and write prayers of remembrance. He should bear witness as the marks he made swirl away into amber water, then drink the diffused prayers—prayers for the lost reeds and prayers for himself, that he be remembered.

Postcard to My Older Self from My Younger Self, Bodega Bay, July 1970

In case you're looking for me, I'm fine. I'm where you left me, in front of the half-moon window framed in cerulean blue, in the skinny-legged cottage that stilt-walked itself up against sand dunes and tall grass shimmering in gin-and-tonic breezes. Always the optimist, I invited Marcel Proust along on this honeymoon. I see now this is no time for remembering things past or searching for lost time. My groom and I have scant history together but seas of time before us, limitless, undulating waves of time waiting to be found, moments tumbling over themselves, upending us, propelling us. Proust lies unread, tossed beside the unfolded road map and the unmade bed with tangled sheets hastily plucked from the pile of unopened wedding presents.

Does sea air still make you ravenous? I'm like the greedy guest at the wedding feast, who, having picked the carcass clean, wipes her mouth daintily and proclaims: I wish it were the beginning.

About the Author

Ellen Estilai

Ellen Estilai is a writer and artist living in Riverside, CA. She has spent much of her career collaborating with artists, writers and agencies to strengthen communities through the arts. Ellen has served as the executive director of the Riverside Arts Council and the Arts Council for San Bernardino County and has taught in universities in Iran and California. Her essay "Front Yard Fruit," originally published in *Alimentum*, is included in *New California Writing* 2011 and was selected as a notable essay in The Best

Photo credit: Ali Estilai

American Essays 2011. A Pushcart and Orison prize nominee, she has published poetry, essays and fiction in Phantom Seed; Broad!; Snapdragon; Ink & Letters; Heron Tree; (In)Visible Memoirs 2; HOME: Tall Grass Writers Guild Anthology; Writing from Inlandia; SHARK REEF and Lady Liberty Lit among others. She is the author of *Exit Prohibited,* a memoir of Iran (Inlandia Books, 2023). Because Ellen and her husband have been immigrants in each other's native countries, her writing frequently explores the joys and tribulations of the immigrant experience.

Acknowledgements

The author wishes to thank Jo Scott-Coe and Stephane Barbé Hammer, in whose Inlandia Institute workshops many of these pieces were created.

"On Indefinite Loan to the Universe: Selections from the Permanent Collection, Museum of Missing Things" originally appeared in *Invisible Memoirs*, vol. 2 (2013) and the online journal *Snapdragon: A Journal of Art and Healing* (Winter 2015).

"Persian Lessons" originally appeared in the Summer 2018 issue of SHARK REEF: A Literary Magazine. It contains excerpts from several chapters of *Exit Prohibited: A Memoir,* Inlandia Books, October 2023.

"Walk-Ons" originally appeared in *Writing from Inlandia* 2016.

"Saffron Prayers" first appeared in *Writing from Inlandia* 2016 and was reprinted in *Riddled with Arrows*, Issue 2.3, November 2018.

"Elegy for Cosmo Cool Cat" originally appeared in *Writing from Inlandia* 2017.

Volcanic Interruptions
by Adela Najarro
and Janet Trenchard

Soundcheck
by Elisa Grajeda-Urmston
and Tamara Adams

Sirens in Her Belly
by Romaine Washington

Expansions
by Micah Tasaka

Soul Sister Revue:
A Poetry Compilation
by Cynthia Manick

Gathering the Waters
by Keisha-Gaye Anderson

Maroon
by Angela Peñaredondo

Sarankara Collage
by Madonna Lavon Camel

Jamii is community. At Jamii Publishing we believe that poetry is not a solitary art.
Poetry is an art form that brings people together.
www.jamiipublishing.com
Jamii Publishing is a 501(c)(3) Charitable Organization

Made in the USA
Middletown, DE
06 January 2024